EDGE
BOOKS™

West Highlands, Scotties, and Other

TERRIERS

by Tammy Gagne

CAPSTONE PRESS
a capstone imprint

Edge Books are published by Capstone Press,
1710 Roe Crest Drive, North Mankato, Minnesota 56003
www.mycapstone.com

Library of Congress Cataloging-in-Publication Data
Names: Gagne, Tammy, author.
Title: West Highlands, Scotties, and other terriers / by Tammy Gagne.
Description: North Mankato, Minnesota : Capstone Press, [2017] | Series: Dog
    encyclopedias | Audience: Ages 9-12. | Audience: Grades 4 to 6. | Includes
    bibliographical references and index. | Description based on print version record and
    CIP data provided by publisher; resource not viewed.
Summary: Informative text and vivid photos introduce readers to various terrier
    dog breeds.
Identifiers: LCCN 2015045573 (print) | LCCN 2015043106 (ebook) |
    ISBN 978-1-5157-0304-4 (library binding) | ISBN 978-1-5157-0313-6 (ebook pdf)
Subjects: LCSH: Terriers—Juvenile literature. | Dog breeds—Juvenile literature.
Classification: LCC SF429.T3 (print) | LCC SF429.T3 G34 2017 (ebook) |
    DDC 636.755—dc23
LC record available at http://lccn.loc.gov/2015045573

Editorial Credits
Alesha Halvorson, editor; Terri Poburka, designer; Kelly Garvin, media researcher;
Katy LaVigne, production specialist

Photo Credits
Newscom/Chris Brignell/Photoshot, 12 (bottom); Shutterstock: Allison Herreid, cover
(bottom right), Ammit Jack, 4-5, Andreas Gradin, 28 (top), AnetaPics, 6 (t), Bildagentur
Zoonar GmbH, 18 (t), Ca, 13 (t), callalloo, 20 (t), Capture Light, 8 (t), 11 (t), 15 (t), 21 (t),
cynoclub, 15 (b), 22 (b), Dmitry Kalinovsky, 6 (b), dogist, 16 (t), eAlisa, 20 (b), Eric Isselee,
cover (left), backcover, 7 (b), 10 (b), 11 (b), 18 (b), 21 (b), 23 (b), 24 (b), Erik Lam, 8 (b), 9 (b),
26 (b), 27 (b), Hamik, 7 (t), Jagodka, 16 (b), 28 (b), Joy Prescott, 25 (t), Lenkadan, 17 (t), lev
radin, 9 (t), Lipowski Milan, 13 (b), Marlonneke Willemsen, 14 (b), Nata Sdobnikova, 29
(b), Natalia V Guseva, 23 (t), Nikolai Tsvetkov, cover (br), 26 (t), Olga_i, cover (top right),
photocell, 27 (t), picsbyst, 19 (t), Pukhov Konstantin, cover (top right), rebeccaashworth,
1, Richard Chaff, 24 (t), Robynrg, 25 (b), Susan Schmitz, 19 (b), Svetlana Valoueva, 10 (t),
22 (t), violetblue, 17 (b), 29 (t), VKarlov, 14 (t); Superstock/Marka/Marka, 12 (t)

Printed and bound in the United States of America.
009676F16

Table of Contents

Independent Terriers

The American Kennel Club's (AKC) terrier group is made up of 30 dog breeds. Terriers were first developed as hunting dogs. Many of them worked alongside larger hunting dogs, such as hounds. The hounds chased foxes and other burrowing animals into their dens. The terriers' job was to force **quarry** out of these tight spaces. Some terriers still perform this work.

Many members of the terrier group are popular as pets. These high-energy canines are known for their feisty personalities. They need owners who are prepared to train these intelligent yet independent animals. Pet terriers need lots of exercise and engaging activities.

Terriers have a distinctive, spirited personality. They typically have a low tolerance for other animals, including other dogs. Terriers should never be kept in the same home with small pets, such as mice or hamsters.

Terriers come in a wide range of sizes and appearances. Don't let the littlest group members fool you, though. Every member of the terrier group shares at least some of that determined terrier spirit. Get ready for a look at each one!

FUN FACT

The AKC sponsors dog shows across the United States. At some AKC events, kids can show dogs. Junior handler classes allow children ages 9 to 18 to learn about showing dogs firsthand.

Airedale Terrier

Appearance:

Height: 22 to 24 inches (56 to 61 centimeters)
Weight: 50 to 60 pounds (23 to 27 kilograms)

The Airdale Terrier is the largest member of its AKC group. It has a double-layered coat. The wiry hair is tan with black around the dog's body and neck.

Personality: Few dogs possess a wider range of traits than the Airedale Terrier. This breed is often described as playful to the point of being silly. At the same time, Airedales make excellent guard dogs. Some even served as military dogs in World War I (1914–1918).

Breed Background: The Airdale Terrier is thought to have originated in England in the Aire River Valley. It was developed by crossing a Terrier with an Otterhound.

Country of Origin: England

Recognized by AKC: 1888

Training Notes: The Airedale Terrier becomes bored easily. Owners must be ready to provide these intelligent animals with plenty of positive training and exercise.

Care Notes: Airedale Terriers aren't heavy shedders. However, owners must hand-strip their dogs three to four times per year. By pulling at the coat in a special way, they remove the dead hair. These dogs also enjoy daily exercise, including walks.

FUN FACT

The Airedale Terrier has been nicknamed the King of Terriers.

FAMOUS DOGS

One might say the Airedale Terrier is a presidential breed. Woodrow Wilson's Airedale Terrier, Davy, and Calvin Coolidge's Airedale, Paul Pry, lived in the White House during their owner's terms.

American Staffordshire Terrier

Appearance:

Height: 17 to 19 inches (43 to 48 cm)
Weight: 50 to 70 pounds (23 to 32 kg)

An American Staffordshire Terrier's short coat can be any color, including black, red, and white. It has an athletic build, a stocky body, and strong cheekbones.

Personality: American Staffordshire Terriers are loyal and loving dogs. Called the Am Staff for short, some people think these dogs are natural clowns. They get along well with children and other pets if properly trained.

Breed Background: The Am Staff descends from Bulldogs in England. During the early 1200s, Bulldogs were bred for baiting bulls, which means to annoy or harass a bull for entertainment. Bull-baiting was outlawed in 1835.

Country of Origin: United States

Recognized by AKC: 1936

Training Notes: American Staffordshire Terriers need responsible owners who are willing to train and **socialize** them properly. Training Am Staffs requires patience.

Care Notes: Am Staffs have powerful jaws, so strong chew toys are a must. If you give this dog a soft squeak toy, it will likely destroy the toy in record time.

FUN FACT

The word "American" was added to the American Staffordshire Terrier's name in 1972.

FAMOUS DOGS

Petey from the *Little Rascals* movies was an American Staffordshire Terrier.

Border Terrier

Appearance:

Height: 10 to 11 inches (25 to 28 cm)

Weight: 11 to 16 pounds (5 to 7 kg)

The Border Terrier has a short, wiry coat. Its coat color comes in several varieties, such as wheat, red, blue and tan, dark brown, or black and tan.

Personality: Border Terriers are affectionate dogs and love spending time with their favorite humans. However, they can be easily excited and may bark often.

Breed Background: In the 1800s Borders were used to hunt foxes, otters, and even badgers. The breed barks to drive wild animals from their dens.

Countries of Origin: Scotland, England

Recognized by AKC: 1930

Training Notes: Border Terriers learn quickly and respond well to **obedience** training. Owners should keep training fun as this breed gets bored easily.

Care Notes: A sturdy fence is a must. Borders are skilled escape artists. Their coats are easy to maintain with scissors for quick trims to tidy up their appearance. Their **weatherproof** coats require occasional brushing.

Bull Terrier

Appearance:

Height: 21 to 22 inches (53 to 56 cm)
Weight: 50 to 70 pounds (23 to 32 kg)

Bull Terriers have a unique look. Some people describe the Bull Terrier's head as egg-shaped. The dog is also said to have a Roman nose, which means it has a high bridge. The Bull Terrier has eyes shaped like triangles. Its short, glossy coat comes in many color variations.

Personality: These active dogs are known for their fun personalities. With proper obedience training, Bull Terriers do well in homes with younger kids.

Country of Origin: England

Recognized by AKC: 1885

Training Notes: The Bull Terrier's intelligence is a plus for training. This breed responds best to training when motivated by toys or treats.

Care Notes:

Daily exercise is important for Bull Terriers. They require occasional grooming with a soft brush or a hound glove, which is a mitt with brush bristles.

▲ FAMOUS DOGS

Bullseye, the mascot for the retailer Target, is a Bull Terrier. The red circles around her left eye are Humane Society-approved vegetable dye and are only placed on her face for advertisements.

FUN FACT

A smaller dog called the Miniature Bull Terrier is considered a separate breed. The only difference between the two breeds is size.

Cairn Terrier

Appearance:
Height: 11 to 12 inches (28 to 30 cm)
Weight: 14 to 16 pounds (6 to 7 kg)

Cairn Terriers are built for the outdoors. Their wiry coats resist water and protect the dogs from harsh weather.

Personality: Cairn Terriers are little dogs with big personalities. These tiny canines are as brave, smart, and confident as many larger breeds. They also aren't afraid to demand attention from their owners.

Breed Background: The Cairn Terrier is the smallest of the Scottish terriers. These terriers were developed to hunt rodents. Cairns are piles of stones used as tombstones in Scotland. The Cairn Terrier got its name by driving rats and other tiny creatures out of these rock piles.

Country of Origin: Scotland

Recognized by AKC: 1913

Training Notes: The Cairn Terrier is highly intelligent and can learn quickly. However, even the best-trained Cairns cannot be trusted to obey off leash because they tend to be independent.

Care Notes: This breed should be exercised regularly to stay busy. Its coat should be brushed regularly.

Dandie Dinmont Terrier

Appearance:
Height: 8 to 11 inches (20 to 28 cm)
Weight: 18 to 24 pounds (8 to 11 kg)

The Dandie Dinmont Terrier has a large, fluffy head. Its coat contains a mixture of soft and hard hairs. The Dandie Dinmont comes in either mustard, which is a yellow-tan, or pepper, which is a black and white mix.

Personality: The Dandie Dinmont Terrier isn't as hyper as some other small dogs. They love to cuddle with their favorite humans.

Breed Background: The Dandie Dinmont was developed in the Cheviot Hills between England and Scotland in the 1700s.

Areas of Origin: Scotland, England

Recognized by AKC: 1886

Training Notes: If an owner wants a Dandie with a mild personality, training is important. Dandie owners will get the best results with positive, rewards-based training.

Care Notes: This breed needs a large amount of grooming, including regular brushing. Daily exercise, such as playing in a fenced area or a walk on a leash, is important.

FUN FACT

The Dandie Dinmont is the only AKC breed named after a fictional character. The name came from Sir Walter Scott's novel, *Guy Mannering.* The character Mr. Dandie Dinmont owned small Scottish terriers.

FAMOUS DOGS

England's Queen Victoria owned a Dandie Dinmont Terrier.

Glen of Imaal Terrier

Appearance:

Height: 12 to 14 inches (30 to 36 cm)
Weight: up to 35 pounds (16 kg)

The Glen of Imaal Terrier has a medium-length double coat. The hair comes in several shades, including wheaten, blue, or brindle. The color brindle means brown with streaks of another color.

Personality: Glens adore their owners. They want to be with people as much as possible. At the same time, these dogs aren't nearly as demanding as other terrier breeds.

Breed Background: The Glen of Imaal Terrier is named for a glen, or valley, in Ireland's Wicklow Mountains. The Irish Kennel Club recognized the breed in 1934. But it would be decades before the Kennel Club of England or the AKC would follow.

Country of Origin: Ireland

Recognized by AKC: 2004

Training Notes: Glens learn quickly. They also bore quickly. The key to training this breed is keeping the sessions short and interesting.

Care Notes: Glen of Imaal Terriers need a surprising amount of exercise and **stimulation**. Owners should be prepared to go for long walks and play plenty of games. They must also be patient when it comes to locating a puppy. Because there aren't many breeders, wait lists are common.

FUN FACT

Glen of Imaal Terriers mature slower than many other breeds. Glens often aren't considered adults until they are 3 or 4 years old.

Irish Terrier

Appearance:

Height: 15 to 19 inches (38 to 48 cm)
Weight: 25 to 27 pounds (11 to 12 kg)

At first glance the Irish Terrier looks a lot like the Airedale Terrier. The biggest difference is size. The Irish Terrier is smaller than the Airedale. The Irish Terrier is also red instead of black and tan.

Personality: Like most other terriers, the Irish Terrier's hunting instinct is strong. These dogs are also highly affectionate and protective.

Country of Origin: Ireland

Recognized by AKC: 1885

Training Notes: The Irish Terrier is intelligent yet requires patience to train. Even after this dog learns commands, its owners must be consistent and practice them often with the dog.

Care Notes: Irish Terriers need their wiry coats brushed regularly. Owners must be willing to provide these dogs with plenty of exercise, such as daily walks.

FUN FACT

The Irish Terrier earned its nickname the Red Devil from its relentless pursuit of quarry.

Kerry Blue Terrier

Appearance:
Height: 18 to 20 inches (46 to 51 cm)
Weight: 33 to 40 pounds (15 to 18 kg)

The Kerry Blue Terrier is best known for its blue-gray coat. The breed also sports a distinctive mop of hair and beard that give its face a unique shape.

Personality: This breed loves people. It gets along well with both adults and children. When strangers come around, however, it may become protective. Kerry Blue Terriers make excellent guard dogs. While no terrier can be trusted with small animals, this breed isn't a good choice for a multi-pet household.

Country of Origin: Ireland

Recognized by AKC: 1922

Training Notes: This breed is likely to act aggressively with other dogs. Socialization can instill good manners for when the Kerry Blue encounters fellow canines in public. Still, owners should always remain watchful.

Care Notes: Keep a towel handy if you own this breed. The beard of hair absorbs a lot of water each time this dog gets a drink. The Kerry Blue Terrier's non-shedding coat is **hypoallergenic** but still needs to be brushed weekly.

FUN FACT

Similar to the Irish Terrier's Red Devil nickname, the Kerry Blue Terrier is often called the Blue Devil.

Manchester Terrier

Appearance:

Height: 15 to 16 inches (38 to 41 cm)
Weight: 12 to 22 pounds (5 to 10 kg)

A quick look might lead a person to mistake a Manchester Terrier for a small Doberman Pinscher. Their coats share the same black and tan coloration. Their pointed ears also make the animals look similar.

Personality: The Manchester's personality is all terrier. These little dogs are lively, loyal, and intelligent. Like other terriers, the Manchester should be introduced slowly to other dogs and strangers.

Country of Origin: England

Recognized by AKC: 1887

Training Notes: Although this is a smart breed, many owners find Manchester Terriers difficult to housetrain. Using a crate and sticking to a strict training schedule can help.

Care Notes: Owners must keep up with this energetic breed. Many find that organized activities, such as **agility** and rally events, help keep this breed entertained.

FUN FACT

A smaller version of this dog is part of the AKC Toy Group.

Miniature Schnauzer

Appearance:
Height: 12 to 14 inches (30 to 36 cm)
Weight: 13 to 15 pounds (6 to 7 kg)

The Miniature Schnauzer has a wiry coat. It comes in solid black, salt and pepper, and black and silver. These dogs also have a bushy beard and eyebrows.

Personality: A Miniature Schnauzer loves its human family members dearly. An excellent watchdog, this breed will bark to alert its owners of approaching strangers.

Country of Origin: Germany

Recognized by AKC: 1926

Training Notes: Trainers rank the Miniature Schnauzer among the smartest dog breeds. They are capable of learning complex commands. They also have incredible enthusiasm for learning new things.

Care Notes: Caring for a Mini Schnauzer involves a lot of time. This dog's coat, including that famous mustache, needs weekly brushing. A Mini Schnauzer needs room to run, so a fenced yard is ideal for this breed.

FUN FACT
The Miniature Schnauzer is the most popular pet among the three Schnauzer breeds.

Norwich Terrier

Appearance:
Height: less than 10 inches (25 cm)
Weight: 10 to 13 pounds (5 to 6 kg)

The Norwich Terrier has short legs and a rough double coat. The hair comes in a variety of colors. A combination of black and tan is among the most popular.

Personality: Norwich Terriers make great pets because they are friendly and loyal. This breed's small size can be deceiving, though. This friendly animal is no lap dog. The Norwich Terrier doesn't want to sit quietly and watch what's happening. It thrives on activity.

Country of Origin:
United Kingdom

Recognized by AKC: 1936

Training Notes: Norwich Terriers are intelligent and easily trained. These dogs respond well to positive reinforcement, such as small treats.

Care Notes: A Norwich Terrier needs regular grooming. Like the Airedale Terrier, the Norwich's fur must be hand-stripped. Many owners find it easier to hire a groomer for this task.

FUN FACT
The Norwich Terrier and the Norfolk Terrier look a lot alike. The only difference is that the Norfolk Terrier has pointed ears instead of floppy ones.

Parson Russell Terrier

Appearance:

Height: 12 to 14 inches (30 to 36 cm)

Weight: 13 to 17 pounds (6 to 8 kg)

Commonly called the Jack Russell Terrier, the Parson Russell comes in two coat types—smooth and broken. Smooth dogs have short hair. The broken coat is a bit longer. Dogs with this coat type have shaggy eyebrows and short beards.

Personality: The Parson Russell Terrier is lively. The breed simply overflows with enthusiasm. Its high activity level makes many people adore the Parson Russell. All that energy is also the reason the breed is not for everyone.

Countries of Origin: England, United States

Recognized by AKC: 1997

Training Notes: This smart dog is capable of learning many commands. Obedience training should begin when the terrier is a puppy.

Care Notes: The Parson Russell Terrier needs to run for at least 30 minutes each day. They are also talented escape artists. The breed is known for getting out of fenced yards by digging under them. Many owners find that **earthdog trials** help fulfill the Parson Russell's needs for exercise, hunting, and digging.

Rat Terrier

Appearance:

Height: 13 to 18 inches (33 to 46 cm)
Weight: 8 to 25 pounds (4 to 11 kg)

Many people describe the Rat Terrier as having large eyes and ears. Part of the reason both body parts look so big is that the rest of the animal is so small.

Personality: Rat Terriers are known for their sweet, playful **temperaments**. These dogs are fiercely loyal and love being watchdogs.

Breed Background: When President Teddy Roosevelt was elected in 1901, the White House had some uninvited guests—rats. Roosevelt's dog Skip helped rid the historic home of the rodents. Because of Skip's outstanding hunting abilities, it is believed that the commander-in-chief gave this dog breed its name.

Country of Origin:

United States

Recognized by AKC: 2013

Training Notes: Many owners find Rat Terriers easier to train than other terrier breeds. These dogs thrive on praise.

Care Notes: Regular exercise is important for these dogs to burn off energy. An occasional bath and brushing will keep Rat Terriers looking their best.

FUN FACT

One Rat Terrier set a record when it cleared a barn of 2,500 rats in just seven hours.

Scottish Terrier

Appearance:
Height: 9 to 11 inches (23 to 28 cm)
Weight: 18 to 22 pounds (8 to 10 kg)

Scottish Terriers have short, stocky bodies. Although they come in several colors, black is the most common.

Personality: Scotties are known for their independence. But they are also gentle and loving with their human family members.

Breed Background: Many dog enthusiasts insist that the Scottish Terrier is the oldest of all the terrier breeds from Scotland. Whether these owners are right about that or not, this dog was the first Scottish breed of the AKC's terrier group.

Country of Origin: Scotland

Recognized by AKC: 1885

Training Notes: Owners can teach this breed a number of commands. But a Scottish Terrier may ignore its training if it doesn't want to comply. Positive praise and rewards may help if this dog develops behavioral problems.

Care Notes: Scotties have a strong chase **instinct**. It is important to keep this breed leashed in public for this reason. Even in the privacy of a backyard, a fence is a good idea for most terriers. A single squirrel can set a Scottie off running.

FUN FACT

President Franklin Roosevelt's Scottie, Fala, had a large following. Some people claim that the White House received more fan mail addressed to this dog than many presidents.

FAMOUS DOGS

Jock from the Disney movie *Lady and the Tramp* is a Scottish Terrier.

Skye Terrier

Appearance:

Height: 9 to 10 inches (23 to 25 cm)
Weight: 25 to 40 pounds (11 to 18 kg)

To people unfamiliar with the breed, the Skye Terrier may look like it needs a haircut. The hair on the breed's head is so long that it falls over the dog's eyes. Its coat is long and silky, flowing all the way to the ground.

Personality: Skye Terrier owners describe the breed as affectionate and loyal. These dogs aren't nearly as warm with new people, however. They are also uneasy around strange dogs.

Breed Background: Developed on the Isle of Skye, this brave little terrier hunted badgers, foxes, and otters. It later became a popular pet for English nobility in the mid-1800s.

Country of Origin: Scotland

Recognized by AKC: 1887

Training Notes: This breed needs early training and socialization. Puppies who are exposed to people will be more comfortable with them as adults.

Care Notes: Skye Terriers need about 30 minutes of exercise each day. A long, daily walk is ideal. Their long hair should be brushed a couple times each week.

FUN FACT

The Skye Terrier has also been called the Clydesdale Terrier, the Glasgow Terrier, and the Paisley Terrier.

21

Smooth Fox Terrier

Appearance:

Height: 13 to 16 inches (33 to 41 cm)

Weight: 15 to 19 pounds (7 to 9 kg)

The Smooth Fox Terrier has a short, smooth coat. It is mostly white with black or tan markings.

Personality: The Smooth Fox Terrier is known for being entertaining and playful. It wants to spend as much time as possible with its family. Left alone too long, this breed can develop behavior problems quickly.

Breed Background: As their name suggests, Smooth Fox Terriers were developed to hunt foxes. Working alongside hounds, these smaller canines could go where the larger dogs could not—in the ground. When the hounds chased a fox into its hole, the terriers would go into the hole and chase quarry back out.

Country of Origin: England

Recognized by AKC: 1885

Training Notes: Training a Smooth Fox Terrier can begin at an early age because of its instinct to hunt. These dogs are intelligent and can learn tricks easily.

Care Notes: Grooming a Smooth Fox Terrier is easy but important. The breed's smooth coat doesn't **mat**. But it does shed heavily twice per year. Weekly brushings can greatly reduce the amount of fur that ends up on carpets and furniture.

Soft Coated Wheaten Terrier

Appearance:

Height: 17 to 19 inches (43 to 48 cm)
Weight: 30 to 40 pounds (14 to 18 kg)

This breed's name is no accident. The Soft Coated Wheaten Terrier's fluffy, tan coat is as soft as silk. A Wheaten's fur also plays a big role in its appearance. The dog's hair hangs over its eyes. The breed also has a long beard.

Personality: Soft Coated Wheaten Terriers offer owners a wide variety of traits. This breed is strong and energetic. Many people describe Wheatens as bouncing clowns. When they aren't on the move, Wheaten Terriers love cuddling with their favorite humans.

Country of Origin: Ireland

Recognized by AKC: 1973

Training Notes:

This breed can be independent. Training goes best with a consistent schedule and firm owner.

Care Notes: Grooming twice per week is necessary. This dog doesn't shed much fur, so owners must brush the dead hair out instead. They also need daily exercise.

FUN FACT

Wheaten Terriers change color as they mature. Puppies are born a rusty brown. The blond wheaten coat develops by the time a dog reaches adulthood.

Staffordshire Bull Terrier

Appearance:

Height: 14 to 16 inches (36 to 41 cm)
Weight: 24 to 38 pounds (11 to 17 kg)

The Staffordshire Bull Terrier is similar in appearance to the American Staffordshire Terrier. The biggest difference between the two breeds is size. The Staffordshire Bull Terrier, or Staffie, is slightly smaller. Its smooth coat comes in up to 14 color variations.

Personality: Staffordshire Bull Terriers are highly affectionate and loyal. Some people also describe these dogs as having a playful sense of humor.

FUN FACT

The Staffordshire Bull Terrier is known for its love and devotion to children in its household. It is nicknamed the "Nanny Dog" for this reason.

Country of Origin: England

Recognized by AKC: 1974

Training Notes: Staffordshire Bull Terriers are known for their intelligence. Positive yet persistent training is a must for this breed, though.

Care Notes: A daily walk and play session are usually enough to keep this dog in good physical shape. Be sure to keep a Staffie leashed at all times in public, however. The breed does not generally get along well with other dogs.

Welsh Terrier

Appearance:
Height: 14 to 15 inches (36 to 38 cm)
Weight: 19 to 21 pounds (9 to 10 kg)

The Welsh Terrier looks a lot like the Airedale Terrier. Its tan and black double coat is wiry on the outside and soft underneath. But the Welsh Terrier is much smaller than the Airedale.

Personality: Most members of the terrier group have lots of energy and a fair amount of independence. Many terrier owners value these traits. For those who do not, however, the Welsh Terrier offers a gentler temperament. Welsh Terriers are calm and mild mannered. Still, they provide plenty of fun and entertainment. They are simply more willing to obey than many of their fellow terrier group members.

Country of Origin: Wales

Recognized by AKC: 1888

Training Notes: Welsh Terriers are smart and easily trainable. However, Welsh Terriers may test their owners' authority, so firm but positive training is a must for these dogs.

Care Notes: Welsh Terriers need about an hour of exercise each day. A fenced yard works great for this breed.

FUN FACT
Because the Welsh Terrier barely sheds, many people who are allergic to dogs can tolerate it.

West Highland White Terrier

FUN FACT

The tips of a West Highland White Terrier's ears are prone to sunburn. Owners can prevent this problem by applying sunscreen before heading outdoors with their pets.

Appearance:

Height: 10 to 11 inches (25 to 28 cm)
Weight: 15 to 21 pounds (7 to 10 kg)

The West Highland White Terrier has a double-layer coat that keeps it warm all year long. Tropical weather is often too much for this furry canine. The Westie is small yet sturdy. One might say these little dogs are strong from head to tail.

Personality: Although they are small, West Highland White Terriers are not lap dogs. They want to do what they please as much as possible.

Breed Background: Determined hunters, Westies have a long history of getting stuck in foxholes. Many owners have had to pull their dogs from these tight spaces—by their tails. Over time the breed has developed an amazingly solid tail.

Country of Origin: Scotland

Recognized by AKC: 1908

Training Notes: Westies are smart and easy to train. However, these dogs should be kept on a leash or in a fenced yard because Westies will run after anything that moves.

Care Notes: To keep a Westie looking its best, daily brushing is important. Frequent baths are also recommended to keep its coat clean. Daily exercise is also necessary for this breed.

Wire Fox Terrier

Appearance:
Height: 13 to 16 inches (33 to 41 cm)
Weight: 15 to 19 pounds (7 to 9 kg)

The Wire Fox Terrier shares many traits with the Smooth Coated Fox Terrier. In fact, the only difference between the two breeds is coat **texture**. A Wire Fox Terrier's dense, wiry coat is mostly white in color with black or tan markings.

Personality: Like their smooth cousins, Wire Fox Terriers are energetic dogs. It doesn't take much to get them moving. Slowing them down, on the other hand, may seem impossible. This lively breed thrives on activity.

Country of Origin: England

Recognized by AKC: 1885

Training Notes: Wire Fox Terriers are highly trainable with positive reinforcement. Like many other terriers, Wire Fox Terriers are independent, so owners must be consistent.

Care Notes: Wire Fox Terriers living in small spaces must get outside for daily exercise. A quick walk won't do. These terriers want to play!

FUN FACT
The Wire Fox Terrier's tail doesn't wag like other dog's tails. Instead, it quivers—moving just slightly back and forth.

27

Other Terrier Breeds

Australian Terrier ▶

Known for: being one of the quieter terriers
Country of Origin: Australia
Recognized by AKC: 1960

Bedlington Terrier

Known for: lamb-like appearance
Country of Origin: England
Recognized by AKC: 1886

Cesky Terrier

Known for: incredible stamina
Country of Origin: Czech Republic
Recognized by AKC: 2011

Lakeland Terrier

Known for: wiry outer coat
Country of Origin: England
Recognized by AKC: 1934

Miniature Bull Terrier

Known for: upbeat and active nature
Country of Origin: England
Recognized by AKC: 1991

....

Norfolk Terrier ▶

Known for: fearlessness
Country of Origin: England
Recognized by AKC: 1979

....

Russell Terrier

Known for: alert and lively nature
Country of Origin: England
Recognized by AKC: 2012

....

Sealyham Terrier ▶

Known for: calm nature
Country of Origin: Wales
Recognized by AKC: 1911

....

Glossary

agility (uh-GI-luh-tee)—the ability to move fast and easily

breed standard (BREED STAN-durd)—the list of ideal traits for a member of a specific dog breed, such as appearance and temperament

earthdog trial (URTH-dawg TRYE-uhl)—a test for small dogs to assess their hunting ability and instincts

hypoallergenic (hye-poh-a-luhr-JEN-ik)—possessing a quality that reduces or eliminates allergic reactions

instinct (IN-stingkt)—behavior that is natural rather than learned

mat (MAT)—a thick, tangled mass of hair

obedience (oh-BEE-dee-uhns)—obeying rules and commands

quarry (KWOR-ee)—an animal hunted as prey

socialize (SOH-shuh-lize)—to train to get along with people and other dogs

stimulate (STIM-yuh-late)—to encourage interest or activity in a person or animal

temperament (TEM-pur-uh-muhnt)—the combination of an animal's behavior and personality; the way an animal usually acts or responds to situations shows its temperament

texture (TEKS-chur)—the way something feels when you touch it

weatherproof (WETH-uhr-proof)—able to withstand exposure to all kinds of weather

Read More

Gagne, Tammy. *Miniature Schnauzer.* Dogs 101. Neptune City, N.J.: TFH Publications, 2015.

Karwoski, Gail. *Terriers: Loyal Hunting Companions.* Hunting Dogs. North Mankato, Minn.: Capstone Press, 2013.

Rustad, Martha E.H. *Dogs.* Little Scientist. North Mankato, Minn.: Capstone Press, 2015.

Internet Sites

FactHound offers a safe, fun way to find Internet sites related to this book. All of the sites on FactHound have been researched by our staff.

Here's all you do:

Visit *www.facthound.com*

Type in this code: 9781515703044

Check out projects, games and lots more at
www.capstonekids.com

Index